The Or

The New English Translation

*All booklets are published thanks to the
generous support of the members of the
Catholic Truth Society*

CATHOLIC TRUTH SOCIETY
PUBLISHERS TO THE HOLY SEE

Contents

THE INTRODUCTORY RITES

The purpose of the Introductory Rites is to ensure that the faithful, who come together as one, establish communion and dispose themselves properly to listen to the Word of God and to celebrate the Eucharist worthily.

General Instruction of the Roman Missal, 46

Before Mass begins, the people gather in a spirit of recollection, preparing for their participation in the Mass. When the people are gathered, the Priest approaches the altar with the ministers and venerates it while the Entrance Chant is sung. All stand during the entrance procession and remain standing until after the Collect prayer which concludes the Introductory Rites.[1]

---

[1] On certain days during the Church's year, for example Palm Sunday and the Easter Vigil, and during certain other celebrations, for example a Funeral Mass, Rite of Entry into the Catechumenate or Baptism, the Introductory Rites take a different form.

Sign of the Cross

*When the Entrance Chant is concluded, the Priest and the
faithful sign themselves with the Sign of the Cross, while
the Priest says:*

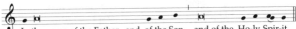

In the name of the Father, and of the Son, and of the Ho-ly Spir-it.

Priest: In the name of the Father, and of the Son,
and of the Holy Spirit.

The people reply:

A-men.

Response: Amen.

Greeting

The Priest greets the people, saying:

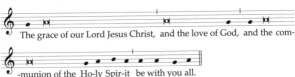

The grace of our Lord Jesus Christ, and the love of God, and the com-

-munion of the Ho-ly Spir-it be with you all.

1. Pr. The grace of our Lord Jesus Christ,
and the love of God,
and the communion of the Holy Spirit
be with you all.

Or:

Grace to you and peace from God our Fa-ther and the Lord Je-sus Christ.

2. Pr. Grace to you and peace from God our Father and the Lord Jesus Christ.

Or:

The Lord be with you.

3. Pr. The Lord be with you.

The people reply:

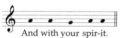

And with your spir-it.

R. And with your spirit.

In this first greeting a Bishop, instead of **The Lord be with you,** *says:* **Peace be with you.**

The Priest, or a Deacon, or another minister, may very briefly introduce the faithful to the Mass of the day.

Penitential Act

There are three forms of the Penitential Act which may be chosen from as appropriate. From time to time on Sundays, especially in Easter Time, instead of the customary Penitential Act, the blessing and sprinkling of water may take place as a reminder of Baptism. Each Penitential Act begins with the invitation to the faithful by the Priest:

Pr. Brethren (brothers and sisters),
   let us acknowledge our sins,
and so prepare ourselves to celebrate the sacred mysteries.

A brief pause for silence follows.

Then all recite together the formula of general confession:
**1. I confess to almighty God
and to you, my brothers and sisters,
that I have greatly sinned,
in my thoughts and in my words,
in what I have done and in what I have failed to do,**
And, striking their breast, they say:

**through my fault, through my fault,
through my most grievous fault;
therefore I ask blessed Mary ever-Virgin,
all the Angels and Saints,
and you, my brothers and sisters,
to pray for me to the Lord our God.**

Or:

2. *The Priest then says:*

Pr. Have mercy on us, O Lord.

The people reply:

R. For we have sinned against you.

The Priest:

Pr. Show us, O Lord, your mercy.

The people:

R. And grant us your salvation.

Or:

3. *The Priest, or a Deacon or another minister, says invocations naming the gracious works of the Lord to which he invites the people to respond, as in the example below:*

Pr. You were sent to heal the contrite of heart:

Lord, have mercy.   *Or:*   Kyrie, eleison.

The people reply:

R. Lord, have mercy.   *Or:*   **Kyrie, eleison.**

The Priest:

Pr. You came to call sinners:

Christ, have mercy.   *Or:*   Christe, eleison.

The people:

R. Christ, have mercy.   *Or:*   **Christe, eleison.**

The Priest:

Pr. You are seated at the right hand of the Father to intercede for us:

Lord, have mercy.   *Or:*   Kyrie, eleison.

The people:

R. Lord, have mercy.   *Or:*   **Kyrie, eleison.**

The absolution by the Priest follows:

Pr. May almighty God have mercy on us,
forgive us our sins,
and bring us to everlasting life.

The people reply:

R. Amen.

The Kyrie, eleison *(Lord, have mercy) invocations follow, unless they have just occurred in a formula of the Penitential Act.*

Pr. Lord, have mercy.	**R. Lord, have mercy.**
Pr. Christ, have mercy.	**R. Christ, have mercy.**
Pr. Lord, have mercy.	**R. Lord, have mercy.**

Or:

Pr. Kyrie, eleison.	**R. Kyrie, eleison.**
Pr. Christe, eleison.	**R. Christe, eleison.**
Pr. Kyrie, eleison.	**R. Kyrie, eleison.**

The Gloria

On Sundays (outside of Advent and Lent), Solemnities and Feast Days, this hymn is either sung or said:

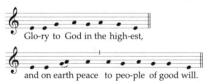

Glo-ry to God in the high-est,

and on earth peace to peo-ple of good will.

We praise you, we bless you, we a-dore you, we glo-ri-fy you,

we give you thanks for your great glo-ry,

Lord God, heav-en-ly King, O God, al-might-y Fa-ther.

Lord Je-sus Christ, On-ly Be-got-ten Son,

Lord God, Lamb of God, Son of the Fa-ther,

you take a-way the sins of the world, have mer-cy on us;

you take a-way the sins of the world, re-ceive our prayer;

you are seat-ed at the right hand of the Fa-ther, have mer-cy on us.

For you a-lone are the Ho-ly One, you a-lone are the Lord,

you a-lone are the Most High, Je-sus Christ, with the Ho-ly Spir-it,

in the glo-ry of God the Fa - ther. A - men.

Glory to God in the highest,
and on earth peace to people of good will.

We praise you,
we bless you,
we adore you,
we glorify you,
we give you thanks for your great glory,
Lord God, heavenly King,
O God, almighty Father.

Lord Jesus Christ, Only Begotten Son,
Lord God, Lamb of God, Son of the Father,
you take away the sins of the world, have mercy on us;
you take away the sins of the world, receive our prayer;
you are seated at the right hand of the Father,
have mercy on us.

For you alone are the Holy One,
you alone are the Lord,
you alone are the Most High,
Jesus Christ,
with the Holy Spirit,
in the glory of God the Father.
Amen.

The Collect

When this hymn is concluded, the Priest, says:

Pr. Let us pray.

And all pray in silence with the Priest for a while.

Then the Priest says the Collect prayer, at the end of which the people acclaim:

R. Amen.

THE LITURGY OF THE WORD

By hearing the word proclaimed in worship, the faithful again enter into the unending dialogue between God and the covenant people, a dialogue sealed in the sharing of the Eucharistic food and drink. The meaning of Communion is proclaimed in the word; the message of Scripture is made actual once again in the Communion banquet. The proclamation of the word is thus integral to the Mass and at its very heart.

Celebrating the Mass, 152

First Reading

Then the reader goes to the ambo and proclaims the First Reading, while all sit and listen.

To indicate the end of the reading, the reader acclaims:

The word of the Lord.

All reply:

R. Thanks be to God.

Following this reading, and the other readings it is appropriate to have a brief time of quiet as those present take the word of God to heart and begin to prepare a prayerful response to what they have heard.

Psalm

The psalmist or cantor sings or says the Psalm, with the people making the response.

Second Reading

On Sundays and certain other days there is a second reading. It concludes with the same response as above.

Gospel

The assembly stands for the Gospel Acclamation to welcome the Gospel. They remain standing in honour of the Gospel reading, the high point of the Liturgy of the Word.

Except during Lent the Gospel Acclamation is:

R. Alleluia,

During Lent the following forms for the Gospel Acclamation are used:

R. Praise to you, O Christ, king of eternal glory!

Or: **R. Praise and honour to you, Lord Jesus!**

Or: **R. Glory and praise to you, O Christ!**

Or: **R. Glory to you, O Christ, you are the Word of God!**

If the Gospel Acclamation is not sung, it may be omitted.

At the ambo the Deacon, or the Priest says:

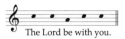

The Lord be with you.

Pr. **The Lord be with you.**

The people reply:

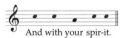

And with your spir-it.

R. **And with your spirit.**

The Deacon, or the Priest:

A reading from the holy Gospel according to | Mat-thew.
                                            | Mark.
                                            | Luke.
                                            | John.

Pr. A reading from the holy Gospel according to N.

He makes the Sign of the Cross on the book and, together with the people, on his forehead, lips, and breast. At the same time the people acclaim:

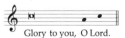

Glory to you, O Lord.

R. **Glory to you, O Lord.**

At the end of the Gospel, the Deacon, or the Priest, acclaims:

The Gospel of the Lord.

Pr. The Gospel of the Lord.

All reply:

Praise to you, Lord Je-sus Christ.

R. **Praise to you, Lord Jesus Christ.**

After the proclamation of the Gospel the congregation is seated to listen to the homily.

The Homily

Then follows the Homily, which is preached by a Priest or Deacon on all Sundays and Holydays of Obligation. On other days, it is recommended. At the end of the Homily it is appropriate for there to be a brief silence for recollection. The congregation then stands.

The Creed

On Sundays and Solemnities, the Profession of Faith will follow. On most occasions the form used is that of the Niceno-Constantinopolitan Creed. However, especially during Lent and Easter Time, the Apostles' Creed may be used.

The Niceno-Constantinopolitan Creed

I believe in one God,
the Father almighty,
maker of heaven and earth,
of all things visible and invisible.

I believe in one Lord Jesus Christ,
the Only Begotten Son of God,
born of the Father before all ages.
God from God, Light from Light,
true God from true God,
begotten, not made, consubstantial with the Father;
through him all things were made.
For us men and for our salvation
he came down from heaven, *(all bow)*
and by the Holy Spirit was incarnate of the Virgin Mary,
and became man.

For our sake he was crucified under Pontius Pilate,
he suffered death and was buried,
and rose again on the third day
in accordance with the Scriptures.
He ascended into heaven
and is seated at the right hand of the Father.
He will come again in glory
to judge the living and the dead
and his kingdom will have no end.

I believe in the Holy Spirit, the Lord, the giver of life,
who proceeds from the Father and the Son,

who with the Father and the Son is adored and glorified,
who has spoken through the prophets.

I believe in one, holy, catholic and apostolic Church.
I confess one Baptism for the forgiveness of sins
and I look forward to the resurrection of the dead
and the life of the world to come. Amen.

The Apostles' Creed

I believe in God,
the Father almighty
Creator of heaven and earth,
and in Jesus Christ, his only Son, our Lord, *(all bow)*
who was conceived by the Holy Spirit,
born of the Virgin Mary,
suffered under Pontius Pilate,
was crucified, died and was buried;
he descended into hell;
on the third day he rose again from the dead;
he ascended into heaven,
and is seated at the right hand of God the Father almighty;
from there he will come to judge the living and the dead.

I believe in the Holy Spirit,
the holy catholic Church,
the communion of saints,
the forgiveness of sins,
the resurrection of the body,
and life everlasting. Amen.

The Prayer of the Faithful (Bidding Prayers)

Various intentions for prayer are introduced by the Deacon or other minister. These will normally be for the Church; for the world; for those in particular need; and for the local community.

After each intention there is a pause while the faithful pray. This time of silent prayer may simply be followed by the next intention, or may be concluded with a sung phrase such as Christ, hear us, *or* Christ graciously hear us, *or by a responsory such as:*

Let us pray to the Lord.

R. Grant this, almighty God.

Or:

R. Lord, have mercy.

Or:

R. Kyrie, eleison.

The Priest concludes the Prayer with a collect.

──The Liturgy of the Eucharist──

For Catholics, the Eucharist is the source and summit of the whole Christian life. It is the vital centre of all that the Church is and does, because at its heart is the real presence of the crucified, risen and glorified Lord, continuing and making available his saving work among us. The Second Vatican Council reminded us: 'the most holy Eucharist holds within itself the whole spiritual treasure of the Church, namely Christ himself, our Passover and our living bread'

Celebrating the Mass, 152

When the Liturgy of the Word has been completed, the people sit and the Offertory Chant begins. It is desirable that the faithful express their participation by making an offering, bringing forward bread and wine for the celebration of the Eucharist and perhaps other gifts to relieve the needs of the Church and of the poor.

Preparatory Prayers

When he has received the bread and wine for the celebration, the Priest, standing at the altar, takes the paten with the bread and holds it slightly raised above the altar with both hands, saying the following words in a low voice:

If, however, the Offertory Chant is not sung, the Priest may speak these words aloud and the people make their response as below:

Pr. Blessed are you, Lord God of all creation,
for through your goodness we have received
the bread we offer you:
fruit of the earth and work of human hands,
it will become for us the bread of life.

When the prayer is said aloud, the people acclaim:

R. Blessed be God for ever.

The Priest then takes the chalice and holds it slightly raised above the altar with both hands, saying in a low voice:

Pr. Blessed are you, Lord God of all creation,
for through your goodness we have received
the wine we offer you:
fruit of the vine and work of human hands,
it will become our spiritual drink.

If, however, the Offertory Chant is not sung, the Priest may speak these words aloud; at the end, the people may acclaim:

R. Blessed be God for ever.

The Priest completes additional personal preparatory rites, and the people rise as he says:

Pr. Pray, brethren (brothers and sisters),
that my sacrifice and yours
may be acceptable to God,
the almighty Father.

The people reply:

**R. May the Lord accept the sacrifice at your hands
for the praise and glory of his name,
for our good
and the good of all his holy Church.**

The Prayer over the Offerings

The Priest says the Prayer over the Offerings, at the end of which the people acclaim:

R. Amen.

The Eucharistic Prayer

The Eucharistic Prayer, the centre and summit of the entire celebration, sums up what it means for the Church to celebrate the Eucharist. It is a memorial proclamation of praise and thanksgiving for God's work of salvation, a proclamation in which the Body and Blood of Christ are made present by the power of the Holy Spirit and the people are joined to Christ in offering his Sacrifice to the Father. The Eucharistic Prayer is proclaimed by the priest celebrant in the name of Christ and on behalf of the whole assembly, which professes its faith and gives its assent through dialogue, acclamations, and the Amen. Since the Eucharistic Prayer is the summit of the Mass, it is appropriate for its solemn nature and importance to be enhanced by being sung.

Celebrating the Mass, 186

V. The Lord be with you.   R. And with your spir-it.

V. Lift up your hearts.   R. We lift them up to the Lord.

V. Let us give thanks to the Lord our God.   R. It is right and just.

Extending his hands, the Priest says:

Pr. The Lord be with you.

The people reply:

R. And with your spirit.

The Priest, raising his hands, continues:

Pr. Lift up your hearts.

The people:

R. We lift them up to the Lord.

The Priest, with hands extended, adds:

Pr. Let us give thanks to the Lord our God.

The people:

R. It is right and just.

The Priest continues with the Preface. Sometimes the Preface will be proper to a particular celebration, sometimes it will be chosen from the selection of those approved for more general use. The Priest concludes the Preface with the people, singing or saying aloud:

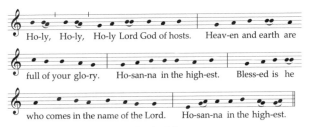

Ho-ly, Ho-ly, Ho-ly Lord God of hosts. Heav-en and earth are full of your glo-ry. Ho-san-na in the high-est. Bless-ed is he who comes in the name of the Lord. Ho-san-na in the high-est.

Holy, Holy, Holy Lord God of hosts.
Heaven and earth are full of your glory.
Hosanna in the highest.
Blessed is he who comes in the name of the Lord.
Hosanna in the highest.

Or:

San-ctus, San-ctus, San-ctus Dó-mi-nus De-us Sá-ba-oth. Ple-ni sunt cæ-li et ter-ra gló-ri-a tu-a. Ho-sán-na in ex-cél-sis. Be-ne-dí-ctus qui ve-nit in nó-mi-ne Dó-mi-ni. Ho-sán-na in ex-cél-sis.

After the singing of the Sanctus the congregation kneels for the remainder of the Eucharistic Prayer.
Texts for the four principal Eucharistic Prayers follow.

Eucharistic Prayer I
(The Roman Canon)

The Priest alone recites:

Pr. To you, therefore, most merciful Father,
we make humble prayer and petition
through Jesus Christ, your Son, our Lord:
that you accept
and bless ✠ these gifts, these offerings,
these holy and unblemished sacrifices,
which we offer you firstly
for your holy catholic Church.
Be pleased to grant her peace,
to guard, unite and govern her
throughout the whole world,
together with your servant N. our Pope
and N. our Bishop,*
and all those who, holding to the truth,
hand on the catholic and apostolic faith.

Commemoration of the Living.

Remember, Lord, your servants N. and N.
and all gathered here,
whose faith and devotion are known to you.
For them, we offer you this sacrifice of praise
or they offer it for themselves
and all who are dear to them:

---

* Mention may be made here of the Coadjutor Bishop, or Auxiliary Bishops.

for the redemption of their souls,
in hope of health and well-being,
and paying their homage to you,
the eternal God, living and true.

Within the Action.

† In communion with those whose memory we venerate,
especially the glorious ever-Virgin Mary,
Mother of our God and Lord, Jesus Christ, †
and blessed Joseph, her Spouse,
your blessed Apostles and Martyrs,
Peter and Paul, Andrew,
(James, John,
Thomas, James, Philip,
Bartholomew, Matthew,
Simon and Jude;
Linus, Cletus, Clement, Sixtus,
Cornelius, Cyprian,
Lawrence, Chrysogonus,
John and Paul,
Cosmas and Damian)
and all your Saints;
we ask that through their merits and prayers,
in all things we may be defended
by your protecting help.
(Through Christ our Lord. Amen.)

---

† Alternative texts are provided for the opening lines of the *Communicantes* ('In communion with those...') according to the feast or season.

Pr. Be pleased, O God, we pray,
to bless, acknowledge,
and approve this offering in every respect;
make it spiritual and acceptable,
so that it may become for us
the Body and Blood of your most beloved Son,
our Lord Jesus Christ.

On the day before he was to suffer,
he took bread in his holy and venerable hands,
and with eyes raised to heaven
to you, O God, his almighty Father,
giving you thanks, he said the blessing,
broke the bread
and gave it to his disciples, saying:

> 'TAKE THIS, ALL OF YOU, AND EAT OF IT,
> FOR THIS IS MY BODY,
> WHICH WILL BE GIVEN UP FOR YOU.'

In a similar way, when supper was ended,
he took this precious chalice
in his holy and venerable hands,
and once more giving you thanks, he said the blessing
and gave the chalice to his disciples, saying:

> 'TAKE THIS, ALL OF YOU, AND DRINK FROM IT,
> FOR THIS IS THE CHALICE OF MY BLOOD,
> THE BLOOD OF THE NEW AND ETERNAL COVENANT,
> WHICH WILL BE POURED OUT FOR YOU AND FOR MANY
> FOR THE FORGIVENESS OF SINS.
> DO THIS IN MEMORY OF ME.'

The mys-ter-y of faith.

Pr. The mystery of faith.

The people continue, acclaiming:

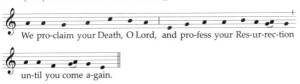

We pro-claim your Death, O Lord, and pro-fess your Res-ur-rec-tion
un-til you come a-gain.

R. **We proclaim your Death, O Lord,**
and profess your Resurrection
until you come again.

Or:

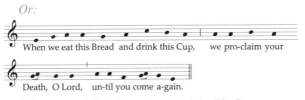

When we eat this Bread and drink this Cup, we pro-claim your
Death, O Lord, un-til you come a-gain.

R. **When we eat this Bread and drink this Cup,**
we proclaim your Death, O Lord,
until you come again.

Or:

Save us, Sav-iour of the world, for by your Cross and Res-ur-rec-tion

you have set us free.

**R. Save us, Saviour of the world,
for by your Cross and Resurrection
you have set us free.**

Then the Priest alone continues:

Pr. Therefore, O Lord,
as we celebrate the memorial of the blessed Passion,
the Resurrection from the dead,
and the glorious Ascension into heaven
of Christ, your Son, our Lord,
we, your servants and your holy people,
offer to your glorious majesty
from the gifts that you have given us,
this pure victim,
this holy victim,
this spotless victim,
the holy Bread of eternal life
and the Chalice of everlasting salvation.

Be pleased to look upon these offerings
with a serene and kindly countenance,
and to accept them,
as once you were pleased to accept
the gifts of your servant Abel the just,
the sacrifice of Abraham, our father in faith,
and the offering of your high priest Melchizedek,
a holy sacrifice, a spotless victim.
In humble prayer we ask you, almighty God:
command that these gifts be borne
by the hands of your holy Angel
to your altar on high
in the sight of your divine majesty,
so that all of us, who through this participation at the altar
receive the most holy Body and Blood of your Son,
may be filled with every grace and heavenly blessing.
(Through Christ our Lord. Amen.)

Commemoration of the Dead

Remember also, Lord, your servants N. and N.,
who have gone before us with the sign of faith
and rest in the sleep of peace.

Grant them, O Lord, we pray,
and all who sleep in Christ,
a place of refreshment, light and peace.
(Through Christ our Lord. Amen.)

To us, also, your servants, who, though sinners,
hope in your abundant mercies,
graciously grant some share
and fellowship with your holy Apostles and Martyrs:
with John the Baptist, Stephen,
Matthias, Barnabas,
(Ignatius, Alexander,
Marcellinus, Peter,
Felicity, Perpetua,
Agatha, Lucy,
Agnes, Cecilia, Anastasia)
and all your Saints;
admit us, we beseech you,
into their company,
not weighing our merits,
but granting us your pardon,
through Christ our Lord.

Through whom
you continue to make all these good things, O Lord;
you sanctify them, fill them with life,
bless them, and bestow them upon us.

*The Priest takes the chalice and the paten with the host
and, raising both, he alone says:*

Through him, and with him, and in him, O God, almighty Father,
in the unity of the Ho-ly Spir-it, all glo-ry and hon-our is yours,
for ev - er and ev-er. R. A-men.

Pr. Through him, and with him, and in him,
O God, almighty Father,
in the unity of the Holy Spirit,
all glory and honour is yours,
for ever and ever.

The people acclaim:

R. Amen.

Then follows the Communion Rite, p. 58.

Eucharistic Prayer II

This Eucharistic Prayer has its own Preface, but it may also be used with other Prefaces, especially those that present an overall view of the mystery of salvation, such as the Common Prefaces. (See p. 28 for Preface dialogue and Sanctus music setting).

Pr. The Lord be with you.

R. And with your spirit.

Pr. Lift up your hearts.

R. We lift them up to the Lord.

Pr. Let us give thanks to the Lord our God.

R. It is right and just.

Pr. It is truly right and just, our duty and our salvation,
always and everywhere to give you thanks, Father most holy,
through your beloved Son, Jesus Christ,
your Word through whom you made all things,
whom you sent as our Saviour and Redeemer,
incarnate by the Holy Spirit and born of the Virgin.

Fulfilling your will and gaining for you a holy people,
he stretched out his hands as he endured his Passion,
so as to break the bonds of death and manifest the resurrection.

And so, with the Angels and all the Saints
we declare your glory,
as with one voice we acclaim:

Holy, Holy, Holy Lord God of hosts.
Heaven and earth are full of your glory.
Hosanna in the highest.
Blessed is he who comes in the name of the Lord.
Hosanna in the highest.

The Priest alone says:

Pr. You are indeed Holy, O Lord,
the fount of all holiness.
Make holy, therefore, these gifts, we pray,
by sending down your Spirit upon them like the dewfall,
so that they may become for us
the Body and ✠ Blood of our Lord Jesus Christ.

At the time he was betrayed
and entered willingly into his Passion,
he took bread and, giving thanks, broke it,
and gave it to his disciples, saying:

'TAKE THIS, ALL OF YOU, AND EAT OF IT,
FOR THIS IS MY BODY,
WHICH WILL BE GIVEN UP FOR YOU.'

In a similar way, when supper was ended,
he took the chalice
and, once more giving thanks,
he gave it to his disciples, saying:

'TAKE THIS, ALL OF YOU, AND DRINK FROM IT,

FOR THIS IS THE CHALICE OF MY BLOOD,

THE BLOOD OF THE NEW AND ETERNAL COVENANT,

WHICH WILL BE POURED OUT FOR YOU AND FOR MANY

FOR THE FORGIVENESS OF SINS.

DO THIS IN MEMORY OF ME.'

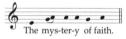
The mys-ter-y of faith.

Pr. The mystery of faith.

The people continue, acclaiming:

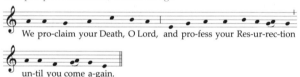
We pro-claim your Death, O Lord, and pro-fess your Res-ur-rec-tion un-til you come a-gain.

**R. We proclaim your Death, O Lord,
and profess your Resurrection
until you come again.**

Or:

When we eat this Bread and drink this Cup, we pro-claim your Death, O Lord, un-til you come a-gain.

**R. When we eat this Bread and drink this Cup,
we proclaim your Death, O Lord,
until you come again.**

Or:

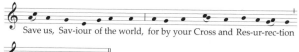

Save us, Sav-iour of the world, for by your Cross and Res-ur-rec-tion

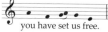

you have set us free.

**R. Save us, Saviour of the world,
for by your Cross and Resurrection
you have set us free.**

Then the Priest alone continues:

Pr. Therefore, as we celebrate
the memorial of his Death and Resurrection,
we offer you, Lord,
the Bread of life and the Chalice of salvation,
giving thanks that you have held us worthy
to be in your presence and minister to you.

Humbly we pray
that, partaking of the Body and Blood of Christ,
we may be gathered into one by the Holy Spirit.

Remember, Lord, your Church,
spread throughout the world,
and bring her to the fullness of charity,
together with N. our Pope and N. our Bishop*
and all the clergy.

---

* Mention may be made here of the Coadjutor Bishop, or Auxiliary Bishops.

In Masses for the Dead, the following may be added:

Remember your servant N.,
whom you have called (today)
from this world to yourself.
Grant that he (she) who was united with your Son
   in a death like his,
may also be one with him in his Resurrection.
Remember also our brothers and sisters
who have fallen asleep in the hope of the resurrection,
and all who have died in your mercy:
welcome them into the light of your face.
Have mercy on us all, we pray,
that with the Blessed Virgin Mary, Mother of God,
with the blessed Apostles,
and all the Saints who have pleased you throughout the ages,
we may merit to be coheirs to eternal life,
and may praise and glorify you
through your Son, Jesus Christ.

The Priest takes the chalice and the paten with the host and, raising both, he alone says:

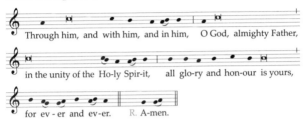

Through him, and with him, and in him, O God, almighty Father,

in the unity of the Ho-ly Spir-it, all glo-ry and hon-our is yours,

for ev-er and ev-er.   R. A-men.

Through him, and with him, and in him,
O God, almighty Father,
in the unity of the Holy Spirit,
all glory and honour is yours,
for ever and ever.

The people acclaim:

R. Amen.

Then follows the Communion Rite, p. 58.

Eucharistic Prayer III

The Priest alone says:

Pr. You are indeed Holy, O Lord,
and all you have created
rightly gives you praise,
for through your Son our Lord Jesus Christ,
by the power and working of the Holy Spirit,
you give life to all things and make them holy,
and you never cease to gather a people to yourself,
so that from the rising of the sun to its setting
a pure sacrifice may be offered to your name.
Therefore, O Lord, we humbly implore you:
by the same Spirit graciously make holy
these gifts we have brought to you for consecration,
that they may become the Body and ✠ Blood
of your Son our Lord Jesus Christ,
at whose command we celebrate these mysteries.

For on the night he was betrayed
he himself took bread,
and, giving you thanks, he said the blessing,
broke the bread and gave it to his disciples, saying:

> 'TAKE THIS, ALL OF YOU, AND EAT OF IT,
> FOR THIS IS MY BODY,
> WHICH WILL BE GIVEN UP FOR YOU.'

In a similar way, when supper was ended,
he took the chalice,
and, giving you thanks, he said the blessing,
and gave the chalice to his disciples, saying:

'TAKE THIS, ALL OF YOU, AND DRINK FROM IT,
FOR THIS IS THE CHALICE OF MY BLOOD,
THE BLOOD OF THE NEW AND ETERNAL COVENANT,
WHICH WILL BE POURED OUT FOR YOU AND FOR MANY
FOR THE FORGIVENESS OF SINS.
DO THIS IN MEMORY OF ME.'

The mys-ter-y of faith.

Pr. The mystery of faith.

The people continue, acclaiming:

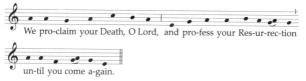

We pro-claim your Death, O Lord, and pro-fess your Res-ur-rec-tion
un-til you come a-gain.

**R. We proclaim your Death, O Lord,
and profess your Resurrection
until you come again.**

Or:

When we eat this Bread and drink this Cup,   we pro-claim your
Death, O Lord,   un-til you come a-gain.

**R. When we eat this Bread and drink this Cup,
we proclaim your Death, O Lord,
until you come again.**

Or:

Save us, Sav-iour of the world, for by your Cross and Res-ur-rec-tion
you have set us free.

**R. Save us, Saviour of the world,
for by your Cross and Resurrection
you have set us free.**

The Priest alone continues:

Pr. Therefore, O Lord, as we celebrate the memorial
of the saving Passion of your Son,
his wondrous Resurrection
and Ascension into heaven,
and as we look forward to his second coming,
we offer you in thanksgiving
this holy and living sacrifice.

Look, we pray, upon the oblation of your Church
and, recognizing the sacrificial Victim by whose death
you willed to reconcile us to yourself,
grant that we, who are nourished
by the Body and Blood of your Son
and filled with his Holy Spirit,
may become one body, one spirit in Christ.

May he make of us
an eternal offering to you,
so that we may obtain an inheritance with your elect,
especially with the most Blessed Virgin Mary,
    Mother of God,
with your blessed Apostles and glorious Martyrs
(with Saint N.: *the Saint of the day or Patron Saint*)
and with all the Saints,
on whose constant intercession in your presence
we rely for unfailing help.

May this Sacrifice of our reconciliation,
we pray, O Lord,
advance the peace and salvation of all the world.
Be pleased to confirm in faith and charity
your pilgrim Church on earth,
with your servant N. our Pope and N. our Bishop*,
the Order of Bishops, all the clergy,
and the entire people you have gained for your own.
Listen graciously to the prayers of this family,
whom you have summoned before you:

---

* Mention may be made here of the Coadjutor Bishop, or Auxiliary Bishops.

in your compassion, O merciful Father,
gather to yourself all your children
scattered throughout the world.

† To our departed brothers and sisters
and to all who were pleasing to you
at their passing from this life,
give kind admittance to your kingdom.
There we hope to enjoy for ever the fullness of your glory
through Christ our Lord,
through whom you bestow on the world all that is good. †

*The Priest takes the chalice and the paten with the host
and, raising both, he alone says:*

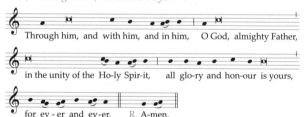

Through him, and with him, and in him, O God, almighty Father,
in the unity of the Ho-ly Spir-it, all glo-ry and hon-our is yours,
for ev-er and ev-er.   R. A-men.

Through him, and with him, and in him,
O God, almighty Father,
in the unity of the Holy Spirit,
all glory and honour is yours,
for ever and ever.

The people acclaim:

R. Amen.

Then follows the Communion Rite, p. **58**.

*When this Eucharistic Prayer is used in Masses for the
Dead, the following may be said:*

† Remember your servant N.
whom you have called (today)
from this world to yourself.
Grant that he (she) who was united with your Son
    in a death like his,
may also be one with him in his Resurrection,
when from the earth
he will raise up in the flesh those who have died,
and transform our lowly body
after the pattern of his own glorious body.

To our departed brothers and sisters, too,
and to all who were pleasing to you
at their passing from this life,
give kind admittance to your kingdom.
There we hope to enjoy for ever the fullness of your glory,
when you will wipe away every tear from our eyes.
For seeing you, our God, as you are,
we shall be like you for all the ages
and praise you without end,
He joins his hands.
through Christ our Lord,
through whom you bestow on the world all that is good. †

Eucharistic Prayer IV

It is not permitted to change the Preface of this Eucharistic Prayer because of the structure of the Prayer itself, which presents a summary of the history of salvation. (See p. 28 for Preface dialogue and Sanctus music setting).

Pr. The Lord be with you.

R. And with your spirit.

Pr. Lift up your hearts.

R. We lift them up to the Lord.

Pr. Let us give thanks to the Lord our God.

R. It is right and just.

Pr. It is truly right to give you thanks,
truly just to give you glory, Father most holy,
for you are the one God living and true,
existing before all ages and abiding for all eternity,
dwelling in unapproachable light;
yet you, who alone are good, the source of life,
have made all that is,
so that you might fill your creatures with blessings
and bring joy to many of them by the glory of your light.

And so, in your presence are countless hosts of Angels,
who serve you day and night
and, gazing upon the glory of your face,
glorify you without ceasing.

With them we, too, confess your name in exultation,
giving voice to every creature under heaven,
as we acclaim:

Holy, Holy, Holy Lord God of hosts.
Heaven and earth are full of your glory.
Hosanna in the highest.
Blessed is he who comes in the name of the Lord.
Hosanna in the highest.

The Priest alone says:

Pr. We give you praise, Father most holy,
for you are great
and you have fashioned all your works
in wisdom and in love.
You formed man in your own image
and entrusted the whole world to his care,
so that in serving you alone, the Creator,
he might have dominion over all creatures.
And when through disobedience he had lost your friendship,
you did not abandon him to the domain of death.
For you came in mercy to the aid of all,
so that those who seek might find you.
Time and again you offered them covenants
and through the prophets
taught them to look forward to salvation.

And you so loved the world, Father most holy,
that in the fullness of time
you sent your Only Begotten Son to be our Saviour.

Made incarnate by the Holy Spirit
and born of the Virgin Mary,
he shared our human nature
in all things but sin.
To the poor he proclaimed the good news of salvation,
to prisoners, freedom,
and to the sorrowful of heart, joy.
To accomplish your plan,
he gave himself up to death,
and, rising from the dead,
he destroyed death and restored life.

And that we might live no longer for ourselves
but for him who died and rose again for us,
he sent the Holy Spirit from you, Father,
as the first fruits for those who believe,
so that, bringing to perfection his work in the world,
he might sanctify creation to the full.

Therefore, O Lord, we pray:
may this same Holy Spirit
graciously sanctify these offerings,
that they may become
the Body and ✠ Blood of our Lord Jesus Christ
for the celebration of this great mystery,
which he himself left us
as an eternal covenant.

For when the hour had come
for him to be glorified by you, Father most holy,
having loved his own who were in the world,
he loved them to the end:
and while they were at supper,
he took bread, blessed and broke it,
and gave it to his disciples, saying:

'TAKE THIS, ALL OF YOU, AND EAT OF IT,
FOR THIS IS MY BODY,
WHICH WILL BE GIVEN UP FOR YOU.'

In a similar way,
taking the chalice filled with the fruit of the vine,
he gave thanks,
and gave the chalice to his disciples, saying:

'TAKE THIS, ALL OF YOU, AND DRINK FROM IT,
FOR THIS IS THE CHALICE OF MY BLOOD,
THE BLOOD OF THE NEW AND ETERNAL COVENANT,
WHICH WILL BE POURED OUT FOR YOU AND FOR MANY
FOR THE FORGIVENESS OF SINS.

DO THIS IN MEMORY OF ME.'

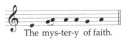
The mys-ter-y of faith.

Pr. The mystery of faith.

The people continue, acclaiming:

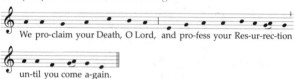

R. **We proclaim your Death, O Lord,**
and profess your Resurrection
until you come again.

Or:

R. **When we eat this Bread and drink this Cup,**
we proclaim your Death, O Lord,
until you come again.

Or:

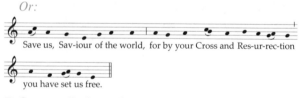

R. **Save us, Saviour of the world,**
for by your Cross and Resurrection
you have set us free.

The Priest alone says:

Pr. Therefore, O Lord,
as we now celebrate the memorial of our redemption,
we remember Christ's Death
and his descent to the realm of the dead,
we proclaim his Resurrection
and his Ascension to your right hand,
and, as we await his coming in glory,
we offer you his Body and Blood,
the sacrifice acceptable to you
which brings salvation to the whole world.

Look, O Lord, upon the Sacrifice
which you yourself have provided for your Church,
and grant in your loving kindness
to all who partake of this one Bread and one Chalice
that, gathered into one body by the Holy Spirit,
they may truly become a living sacrifice in Christ
to the praise of your glory.

Therefore, Lord, remember now
all for whom we offer this sacrifice:
especially your servant N. our Pope,
N. our Bishop,* and the whole Order of Bishops,
all the clergy,
those who take part in this offering,
those gathered here before you,

---

* Mention may be made here of the Coadjutor Bishop, or Auxiliary Bishops.

your entire people,
and all who seek you with a sincere heart.

Remember also
those who have died in the peace of your Christ
and all the dead,
whose faith you alone have known.

To all of us, your children,
grant, O merciful Father,
that we may enter into a heavenly inheritance
with the Blessed Virgin Mary, Mother of God,
and with your Apostles and Saints in your kingdom.
There, with the whole of creation,
freed from the corruption of sin and death,
may we glorify you through Christ our Lord,
through whom you bestow on the world all that is good.

The Priest takes the chalice and the paten with the host and, raising both, he alone says:

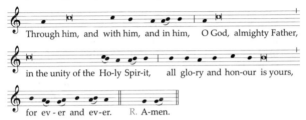

Through him, and with him, and in him, O God, almighty Father,

in the unity of the Ho-ly Spir-it, all glo-ry and hon-our is yours,

for ev-er and ev-er. R. A-men.

Through him, and with him, and in him,
O God, almighty Father,
in the unity of the Holy Spirit,
all glory and honour is yours,
for ever and ever.

The people acclaim:

R. Amen.

Then follows the Communion Rite, p. **58**.

THE COMMUNION RITE

The eating and drinking together of the Lord's Body and Blood in a Paschal meal is the culmination of the Eucharist. The assembly is made ready to share in this banquet by a series of rites that lead from the Eucharistic Prayer directly to the Communion. The themes underlying these rites are the mutual love and reconciliation that are both the condition and the fruit of worthy communion and the unity of the many in the one. These themes are symbolised at both the natural and the sacramental level in the signs of bread and wine now become the Body and Blood of Christ.

Celebrating the Mass, 200

The Lord's Prayer

After the chalice and paten have been set down, the congregation stands and the Priest says:

Pr. At the Saviour's command
and formed by divine teaching,
we dare to say:

Together with the people, he continues:

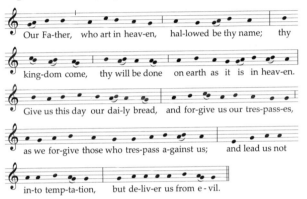

Our Father, who art in heaven,
hallowed be thy name;
thy kingdom come,
thy will be done
on earth as it is in heaven.
Give us this day our daily bread,
and forgive us our trespasses,
as we forgive those who trespass against us;
and lead us not into temptation,
but deliver us from evil.

Or:

Pa-ter nos-ter, qui es in cae-lis: san-cti-fi-cé-tur no-men tu-um;

ad-vé-ni-at reg-num tu-um; fi-at vo-lún-tas tu-a, si-cut in caelo,

et in ter-ra. Pa-nem nos-trum co-ti-di-á-num da no-bis hó-di-e;

et di-mít-te no-bis dé-bi-ta nos-tra, si-cut et nos di-mít-ti-mus

de-bi-tó-ri-bus nos-tris; et ne nos in-dú-cas in ten-ta-ti-ó-nem;

sed lí-be-ra nos a ma-lo.

The Priest alone continues, saying:

De-liver us, Lord, we pray, from every e-vil, graciously grant peace

in our days, that, by the help of your mercy, we may be always free

from sin and safe from all dis-tress, as we a-wait the bless-ed hope

and the coming of our Sav-iour, Je-sus Christ.

Pr. Deliver us, Lord, we pray, from every evil,
graciously grant peace in our days,
that, by the help of your mercy,
we may be always free from sin
and safe from all distress,
as we await the blessed hope
and the coming of our Saviour, Jesus Christ.

The people conclude the prayer, acclaiming:

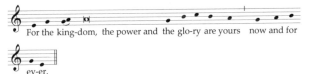

For the king-dom, the power and the glo-ry are yours now and for ev-er.

R. **For the kingdom,**
the power and the glory are yours
now and for ever.

The Peace

Then the Priest says aloud:

Pr. Lord Jesus Christ,
who said to your Apostles:
Peace I leave you, my peace I give you;
look not on our sins,
but on the faith of your Church,
and graciously grant her peace and unity
in accordance with your will.
Who live and reign for ever and ever.

The people reply:

R. Amen.

The Priest, adds:

Pr. The peace of the Lord be with you always.

The people reply:

R. And with your spirit.

Then the Deacon, or the Priest, adds:

Pr. Let us offer each other the sign of peace.

And all offer one another the customary sign of peace: a handclasp or handshake, which is an expression of peace, communion, and charity.

Breaking of the Bread

Then the Priest takes the host, breaks it over the paten, and places a small piece in the chalice, saying quietly:

Pr. May this mingling of the Body and Blood
of our Lord Jesus Christ
bring eternal life to us who receive it.

Meanwhile the following is sung or said:

Lamb of God, * you take a-way the sins of the world,

have mer-cy on us.

Lamb of God, * you take a-way the sins of the world,

have mer-cy on us.

Lamb of God, * you take a-way the sins of the world,

grant us peace.

**Lamb of God, you take away the sins of the world,
have mercy on us.**
**Lamb of God, you take away the sins of the world,
have mercy on us.**
**Lamb of God, you take away the sins of the world,
grant us peace.**

Or:

A-gnus De-i, * qui tol-lis pec-cá-ta mun-di: mi-se-ré-re no-bis.

A-gnus De-i, * qui tol-lis pec-cá-ta mun-di: mi-se-ré-re no-bis.

A-gnus De-i, * qui tol-lis pec-cá-ta mun-di: do-na no-bis pa-cem.

The invocation may even be repeated several times if the fraction is prolonged. Only the final time, however, is **grant us peace** *said. After the Lamb of God, the people kneel.*

Invitation to Communion

After his private prayers of preparation the Priest genuflects, takes the host and, holding it slightly raised above the paten or above the chalice says aloud:

Pr. Behold the Lamb of God,
behold him who takes away the sins of the world.
Blessed are those called to the supper of the Lamb.

And together with the people he adds once:

**R. Lord, I am not worthy
that you should enter under my roof,
but only say the word
and my soul shall be healed.**

While the Priest is receiving the Body of Christ, the Communion Chant begins.

Communion Procession

After the priest has reverently consumed the Body and Blood of Christ he takes the paten or ciborium and approaches the communicants. The communicants come forward in reverent procession. They receive Holy Communion standing and after making a preparatory act of reverence by bowing their head in honour of Christ's presence in the Sacrament.

The Priest raises a host slightly and shows it to each of the communicants, saying:

Pr. The Body of Christ.

The communicant replies:

R. Amen.

And receives Holy Communion.

When Communion is ministered from the chalice the minister of the chalice raises it slightly and shows it to each of the communicants, saying:

Pr. The Blood of Christ.

The communicant replies:

R. Amen.

And receives Holy Communion.

After the distribution of Communion, if appropriate, a sacred silence may be observed for a while, or a psalm or other canticle of praise or a hymn may be sung.

Prayer after Communion

Then, the Priest says:

Pr. Let us pray.

All stand and pray in silence for a while, unless silence has just been observed. Then as the Priest says the Prayer after Communion, at the end of which the people acclaim:

R. Amen.

THE CONCLUDING RITES

After the Communion Rite, the Mass closes with a brief Concluding Rite. Its purpose is to send the people forth to put into effect in their daily lives the Paschal Mystery and the unity in Christ which they have celebrated. They are given a sense of abiding mission, which calls them to witness to Christ in the world and to bring the Gospel to the poor.

Celebrating the Mass, 217

Any brief announcements follow here. Then the dismissal takes place. On certain days or occasions, the formula of blessing which follows will be preceded by another more solemn formula of blessing or by a prayer over the people.

The Priest says:

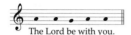

The Lord be with you.

Pr. The Lord be with you.

The people reply:

And with your spir-it.

R. And with your spirit.

The Priest blesses the people, saying:

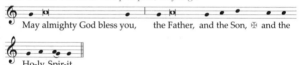

May almighty God bless you,   the Father, and the Son, ✠ and the

Ho-ly Spir-it.

Pr. May almighty God bless you,
the Father, and the Son, ✠ and the Holy Spirit.

The people reply:

A-men.

R. Amen.

In a Pontifical Mass, the celebrant receives the mitre and, extending his hands, says:

Celebrant: The Lord be with you.

All reply:

R. And with your spirit.

The celebrant says:

Cel. Blessed be the name of the Lord.

All reply:

R. Now and for ever.

The celebrant says:

Cel. Our help is in the name of the Lord.

All reply:

R. Who made heaven and earth.

Then the celebrant receives the pastoral staff, if he uses it, and says:

Cel. May almighty God bless you,
the Father, ✠ and the Son, ✠ and the Holy ✠ Spirit.

All:

R. Amen.

*Then the Deacon, or the Priest himself says the Dismissal,
to which in all cases the people reply:* **Thanks be to God.**

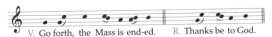

V. Go forth, the Mass is end-ed.   R. Thanks be to God.

Pr. Go forth, the Mass is ended.

Or:

V. Go and an-nounce the Gos-pel of the Lord.   R. Thanks be to God.

Pr. Go and announce the Gospel of the Lord.

Or:

V. Go in peace, glorifying the Lord by your life.   R. Thanks be to God.

Pr. Go in peace, glorifying the Lord by your life.

Or:

V. Go in peace.   R. Thanks be to God.

Pr. Go in peace.

The people reply:

R. Thanks be to God.

*Then the Priest venerates the altar as at the beginning. After
making a profound bow with the ministers, he withdraws.
If any liturgical action follows immediately, the rites of
dismissal are omitted.*